a short guide to
Agile Transformation

Karl Smith

Polymath Knowledge
Edinburgh, Scotland
2021

1.0   Acknowledgements

I'd like to thank so many clients over the last 31 years who have entrusted me to refine and evolve their organisational transformation, capability or service launch and be responsible for their success.

2.0   Dedication

This book is dedicated to quite a lot of people, but mainly to my wife Hazel who has always supported me and given me the confidence to feel I can go against the crowd to do the right thing. To current and former colleagues including Drew Calladine and Rob McHarg, I'm glad that I met you because I learned from you. I'd especially like to thank Sabrina C E Bruce and Robert Bruce for their support and encouragement.

3.0 Table of Contents

4.0　Introduction

The enclosed is not theories but real consultancy refined by the experience of working in enterprises with both business and technology leadership. It is aimed at decision makers and to everyone who has started or is about to start an Agile Transformation.

This short guide to Agile Transformation is a Strategy and Planning book. There are so many moving parts in an Agile Transformation and this book covers them all from a strategic level delving down into tactical information where required to highlight common errors and opportunities. A must read for people getting involved in Agile Transformation.

Agile Transformation is about accepting that businesses are unique and building that into their transformation DNA. Agile Transformation is about gaining freedom, transparency and growth.

"Conformity is the jailer of freedom and the enemy of growth" John Fitzgerald Kennedy, 1961.

4.1　Notes on the Cover Image

In the cover image there is shoal of fish, we are witnessing instinct, but why? Well, it's easier to swim in large groups it reduces friction, so they conserve energy. It also makes it easier to find food and eat. Lastly, it's a defensive position against most predators.

Humans also operate by instinct in work. Large groups of people with a common and agreed way of working creates comfort, it makes life easier knowing how you fit in, even if it's not where you want to be, at least you know.

People have psychological safety in their current ways of working and changing that has a huge impact on their identity, how they relate to their colleagues, their sense of value, their surety around the future all, which impacts their response to change. Your change strategy then determines if you're working with secure adults or insecure and defensive people actively working against the interests of the enterprise.

5.0   About the Author

Karl A L Smith (1966 to present) was born in Kent, grew up in Beckenham and currently lives in Scotland and works globally. He has focused his life on problem solving, to fix the everyday problems of humans.

He has always been fascinated by how technology can augment the lives of humans;

"My desire was not to build things that humans

already do but to find out how technology could evolve our human experience."

He has been named in the Top 100 Thought Leaders and Influencers to follow in 2021 by Thinkers360 and is currently ranked number One Globally by Thinkers360 as the Thought Leader and Influencer for Agile and the Future of Work.

Karl has been involved in voluntary work since his teens and has been a driving force in the formation of many initiatives that are focused on education as a pathway to personal and financial freedoms. He was involved in the creation and operations of the largest online free Agile festival in history with over 800 conferences and events in February 2021 to celebrate 20 years of Agile, Agile20Reflect Festival as a Trustee and CTO, also setting up Access Agile.

Karl A L Smith is a co-founder of Agile World talk show with Sabrina C E Bruce using the name of his consultancy Agile World Inc. (by formal agreement) which was incorporated in 2006 https://agile-world.us/thinking/community-projects/. The voluntary entertainment, media and education ecosystem Agile World https://agile-world.charity/ includes Agile World Broadcast Media https://agile-world.news/ Agile World Institute https://agile-world.institute/ and Agile World Resources which is five separate initiatives joined together into one digital experience https://agile-world.org/ and Think

Agile an agile think tank https://agile-world.info/.
Agile World now Incorporated is based in California
and continues to grow. Agile World Broadcast Media
talk show has been set up along language and
communication lines and is now available on
Amazon as a free podcast
https://www.amazon.co.uk/item_name/dp/B08JK3
MBDL/

Karl is an avid learner and polymath from school to
Ravensbourne College of Art and Design, Middlesex
University and later Napier University his knowledge
sits across design, engineering, science and the
humanities. He is best known for launching new
business capabilities or optimizing existing ones and
provides consultancy service globally.

Karl A L Smith is a prolific writer in spite of his
dyslexia, his blog is widely reposted and syndicated
https://karlsmith.info/. He has been recognised for
his work to date by the British Computer Society
with a Fellowship FBCS.

6.0   Transformation Strategy

Everything starts with the strategy; all businesses
have one and it is essential that any kind of
transformation not only aligns with it but that its
outcomes add towards delivering the overall
strategy. As you work through your transformation
strategy, design, planning and implementation use

the business strategy as a mirror to validate what you're doing and the outcomes you're creating.

The primary strategy for effectual Agile Transformation is that it is done by self-adoption. This adoption must be guided to avoid the creation and adoption of antipatterns, and this is the bases of using external consultancy to plan and deliver the unique guidelines for individual client companies.

6.1   Transformation Patronage

Patronage is such an ancient term of reference, yet it is still essential to success. It defines the ability to be effective, to gain access, to drive viable scope and to deal with anti-patterns. The best person to be the patron of an Agile Transformation is the CEO, but they really need to have a benefits package to share with the board and investors. After the CEO, the CTO/CIO because they have a seat at the top table however this will ultimately play into the battle between business imperatives and technology ones. These are irrelevant for Agile Transformation because it is agnostic and holistic. In fact, the leap from technology into business for any change is counterculture from a business perspective as the insight and strategy for an enterprise is perceived to be owned by the business.

6.2   Agile Transformation Benefits Packages

Agile Transformation benefits packages consist of many things often relative to the specific business domain and markets however common values would include.

- Increase customer acquisition, advocacy and lifetime value
- Improved business agility and ability to rapidly respond to change and opportunity
- Increased credibility, confidence and influence across the business
- Effective delivery against financial targets
- Enabling positive behavioural change
- Fostering a human centric, transparent, trustworthy and agile culture
- Viable, scalable and actionable roadmap to deliver innovation and change
- More consistent and sustainable profitability and business growth
- Successful, timely delivery of evidence based transformative change
- More satisfied and engaged employees with increased retention and productivity
- Builds flexibility into business DNA
- Supports a culture of next best action
- Creates a focus on work that delivers defined value
- Reduces management overhead, bureaucracy and timelines
- Delivers transparent and scalable working practices

- Enables idea to value workflow for executive to customer engagement
- Delivers flexible portfolio management
- Enables continuous and market responsive evolution

Exact returns on investment are difficult to stipulate without a scope definition however there are a number of themes.

- Increased throughput of value creating work (up as much as 60% optimal being 95%) as unplanned work is revealed and dramatically reduced (down as much as 60% optimal being 95%)
- Increased visibility at executive leadership level with new capacity to refocus the entire organisation every three months
- Operational measurement of all work to indicate blockages in the flow of work to provide continuous improvements
- Operational flexibility as the focus moves to skills and teams over time served and individual roles
- Staff galvanization and focus as pay and rewards become team-based assessments and transparent
- Daily risk awareness, status and management for the whole enterprise
- Flattened hierarchy as management becomes systemic by pull rather than push

(though self-organising workflows) giving a 10% to 40% FTE reduction of management and increasing the producer to non-producer ratio (it is essential to see that this is a by-product and not the reason for Agile Transformation else it leads to compromising Organise the Work and will cause Failure).

While not all these values can be promised this list will help you extrapolate a viable list for the CEO, the board of directors and to add to the company statement for investors and analysts to understand the direction of travel and measurable indicators of success. It is essential that all involved and affected understand what is happening and why. This will frame all future understanding and personal appropriation by the executive culture of the transformation.

6.3   Strategic Adjusted Governance

I talk about transformational and operational governance later, but strategic adjusted governance is critical at the outset. If you don't get it your transformation will be crippled by the organisation protecting itself using the mechanism of governance. It's important to understand that governance is an essential line in the sand that stepping over causes multiple policies to be enacted including in many cases contract termination. As a practitioner of ISO/IEC 38500 the international standard for the corporate governance of

information technology I understand that often
Governance is seen as an impediment to
Transformation but really, it's an opportunity if you
know what to ask for, where to ask and from whom.

Agile Transformation in fact requires an agreement
between the existing Governance Framework and
the Transformation to operate and the setting up of
agreed operational interfaces. This agreement
should be widely communicated to avoid
unnecessary confrontation. I will expand on these in
the Transformational to Operational Governance
section.

6.4   Contractual Basis

It is essential to avoid outcome-based contracts with
Agile Transformation as detailed Agile Outcomes
cannot be predetermined. Agile Transformation is
intended to build flexibility into organisations and is
delivered under the same construct. Essentially
outcomes are emergent rather than predictable so
no one can really determine what they will be.
Instead, a stage payment based on proven guiderail
components is better for all involved.

6.5   Change Measurement

There really is no point in doing any kind of
transformation if you can't define the current state
through metrics and measure changes as they are
delivered. It is surprising the number of
organisations still reliant on unchecked subjective

measures made by people into the current state of their business and work areas.

"It is essential to recognise that change without measurement is pointless"

Creating repeatable patterns for measurement in Agile Transformation is essential. Don't get trapped in your thinking about measurement there are valuable structured or unstructured, subjective or objective, qualitative or quantitative measures all of which may be viable to aid different activities in Agile Transformation. But it is essential to understand that Agile measurement is timeline and insight based they are not static and are not continuously reporting either.

Measurement can really be split several ways in a transformation Timeline;

- Current state
- Understanding transformation activities during change
- Emergent measurement
- Understanding transformation maturity (there is no end state) during change, into business as usual and through responding in a flexible manner as needed

Or by Insight;

- Throughput of work (idea to value, or idea to feedback)
- Effectiveness (perceptions or against start measurements)
- Quality (maintain existing, raising standards, levelling quality in both ideas, creation, production, delivery and feedback)
- Customer satisfaction (end customer satisfaction since value is overall value driving from Business Strategy not a department view)
- Reduced support cost (as a secondary output to quality yet primary measure)
- Reduced returns (less bad experience and less returns)
- Actual response to market or situational factors

I have not found any off the shelf solution for measuring Agile Transformation (Governance affords oversight not measurement), there are solutions that focus on technology perhaps because Agile has been present longer there than any other location. However, I have not seen solutions that build flexibility in as core thinking. The most innovative work I have seen to date is from Anthony Coppedge based in the USA. He has been gathering qualitative data from team retrospectives and converting it into quantitative insights through a pattern analysis technique that utilises Artificial Intelligence and dashboard reporting of sales activities. Every indication is that this is the missing link for Business Agility to be measured, refined and actually prove the outcomes being sold to enterprises.

6.5.1   What to Measure

First measure the current state with the existing metrics, think in phases, starting metrics, transition metrics and operational metrics for each transition slice. These metrics roll up to a transformation dashboard but act independently from each other in order to avoid fudging the metrics.

Starting point measurement allows the journey to be monitored and for experiments to be enacted so that course corrections are made on knowledge and not reactions. It is imperative to understand that starting metrics and indicators evolve and are also often discarded.

There is lots of talk around measuring KPI's (key performance indicators) and OKR's (objectives and key results), but it is essential that measurements post start is emergent not directive. So, I'd advise against the use of end point thinking or predetermining KPI's or OKR's.

6.5.2   How to Measure

Change measurement wherever possible should be automated to avoid data tampering that may provide a glossy view of the current or transition state. Measurement is not to determine success it's to understand the current state and to be able to make correctly informed decisions on the next best action.

6.5.3   Cost of Measurement

Measurement is a major piece of work in its own rights and could easily take 20-30% of your entire budget if the data and ways to gather it does not already exist. This budget is not predominantly software it is in fact peoples time to ensure that planning and retro reporting activities are baked into organisations and in the first instance funded by the transformation. People will require a charge code from the transformation to conduct these activities until new budget formats are agreed to cover these new activities.

7.0   Conceptual Design

Before doing anything else it is imperative to agree on the conceptual design, essentially the scope. What is in scope, what is out of scope and what are the grey areas. This takes a few weeks it's not exhaustive, because agile transformation is led by experimentation not absolutes. It is essential to maintain flexibility to opportunity as it arises. This initial work will also indicate quick wins, potential outcomes, value attributes and current dependencies or limitations.

7.1   Transformation Patterns

Transformation patterns are the playbooks of Agile Transformation. They facilitate the first engagements and evolve as living documents as the transformation makes discoveries, makes decisions (which are logged) and manages risk. By logging decisions, it is possible to retrace when a direction proves that it is not viable, ultimately saving on rework and governance issues later. Transformation patterns are used by everyone in the transformation (especially HR, Communications and Consultants) and are the bases of all transformation sign off, governance and BAU. They also assist in surfacing anti-patterns, practices and behaviours.

7.1.1   Horizontal Strategic Transformation

Not every business will be structured like the model below, but I will use the components to describe types of conceptual Agile Target Operating Model ATOM design.

Executive	Enterprise Portfolio
Business	Business Unit Portfolio
Change	Product Group Portfolio
Technology	Product Group Backlog
Customer	Service or Product Value

This model describes four horizontals the most common target for Agile Transformation is Technology. I have also indicated work groupings but not work types, they are described later. Below are a series of models that indicate possible connections between enterprise organisational structures following existing horizontal constructs.

7.1.2 Vertical Strategic Transformation

The below describes a customer journey transformation where then to end customer experience (for product or service grouping slices) is the focus and it is the customer desire and interaction (or transaction) that becomes the critical path and focus of the enterprise however it is structured.

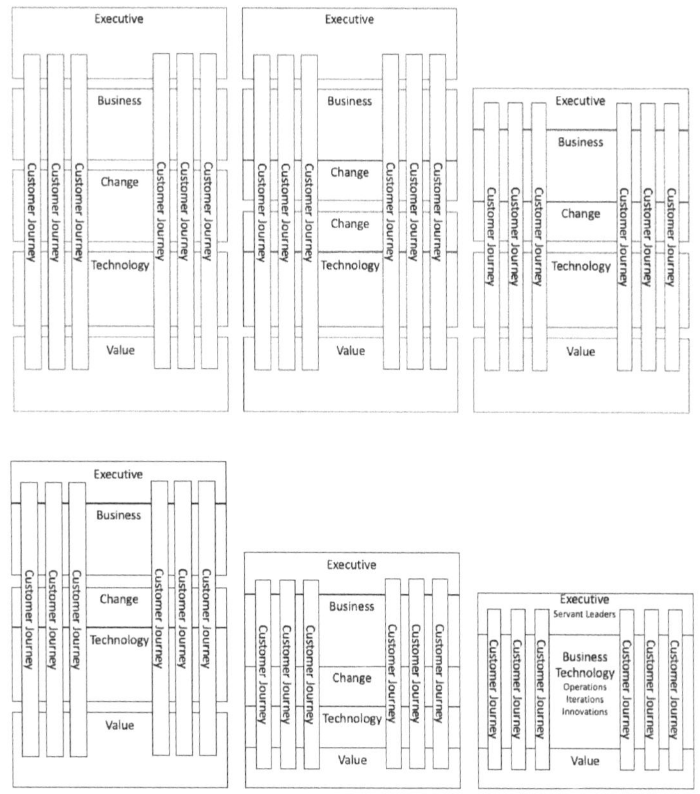

7.1.3   Hybrid Strategic Transformation

Transformation will need to consider a transition hybrid so that the move from old to new ways of working is understood and supported.

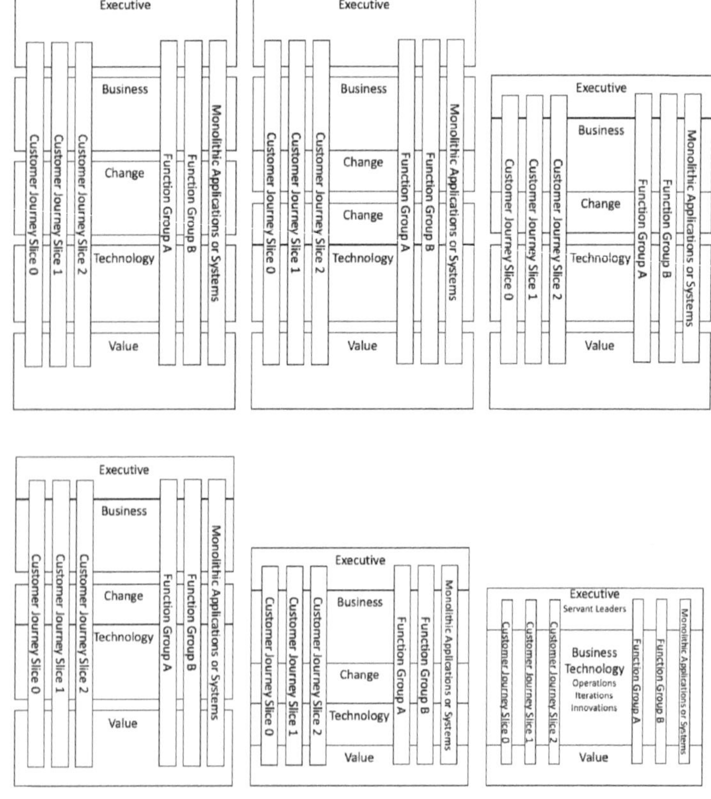

7.1.4   Human Resources Patterns

1. Capability Corporate Strategy and Innovator Skills
2. Capability Measurement and Skills Planning

3. Capability Technical Skills
4. Capability Production or Delivery Skills

7.1.5   Work Patterns

1. Thematic Inception and Outcome Definition
2. Thematic Planning and Theme Allocation
3. Strategic Planning and Backlog Definition
4. Tactical Planning and High-Level Solutions Group, Cross Dependency Release Planning
5. Production Planning and Solutions Delivery Teams
6. Automated Outcome Measurement and Reporting

7.2   Transformation Return on Investment

The lack of a common tool and method to be able to assess Agile Transformation ROI has hindered transformation work for some time. However, with the emergence of the Think Agile (think tank) new agile ideas are surfacing quicker. The Agile Transformation ROI proposes three usages for retrospective transformation spend validation, for go, no go and to deliver return on investment.

7.3   Transformation Anti-patterns

Anti-patterns are a reflection of the patterns except they focus on not delivering transformation. They tend to focus on disabling transformation, perverting transformation, redirecting efforts or funds from transformation. They are common on every transformation. People have become used to being hit by business fads that usually give up, if they fight back. Anti-patterns a really useful to make the patterns better, establish more transparency and by doing so make it clear that everyone is changing, and that the transformation is not just an imposition on one type of employee.

7.3.1   Common Anti-patterns

Rebadging Project Managers (PM) as ScrumMaster (SM), ScrumMaster is an activity not a Role.

SM is not command and control like PM it is a facilitation activity, the Lord is now the Butler. Sadly, the change of mental model required to move from a command-and-control PM to a facilitator SM is too dramatic for many and consequently many Agile Transformations fail at this point because of inflexibility of existing staff forced into new role title they do not agree with and won't perform. Work is pulled from the backlog by the Team collectively not pushed through by a person in Agile, so the SM role is not managerial in the slightest.

Rebadging Programme Managers (PMO) as Agile is highly problematic this role is not required in Agile and is replaced by a Backlog.

The work then exists in software is prioritised by the Product Owner and planned by the whole team not the PO and the SM. The SM facilitates the trajectory set by the team and supports the enforcement of work in progress limits WIP and to stop change requests being injected into the current sprint or backlog without validation including their benefits being logged.

Maintaining Management Structures for HR purposes.

Agile establishes shared team-based management. This leads to Team based assessments validated through automated metrics. HR functions become exception-based activities everything else is community serviced based.

HR maintains existing human capital management processes.
Existing HR processes no longer map to how people are valued or assessed and so how they should be paid.

Staff contracts are not changed the reflect Agile practices and evaluation criteria.

Changing how people work breaches people existing contracts and will require engagements with them and their unions. Ultimately however the way Agile devolves decision making to skilled workers it in fact elevates those workers and when understood is rarely challenged.

<s>The Backlog has not been structure by Weighted Shortest Job First (WSJF).</s> Don't bother focus on Economic Ordering instead WSJF is too subjective

Without doing the right work at the right time in the right order nothing really changes in an enterprise and the Agile Transformation does not deliver a major business benefit.

Work is not in the right format for the Team but there is an expectation they will fix it as they go.

This is an Agile myth the proper response is to return it to the backlog until it is in the right format, with enough detail.

There are so many it probably needs a book all of its own.

8.0   Agile Target Operating Model (ATOM)

The essential outcome of the Conceptual Design work is to collate these concepts into an Agile Target Operating Model (ATOM), with defined components for every aspect of your organisation. And like the chemical element your ATOM will provide the building block for your governance, strategy, finance, legal, technology, human resources, vendor relationships, production, customer service etc. However, the ATOM does not define an end state, because it is used as a current state interrogation tool and not a roadmap. It should evolve based upon the progression of the transformation with common activities to be adopted across the organisation and unique patterns that are monitored to avoid them becoming antipatterns.

There are several benefits to creating an ATOM as it helps with defining boundaries, risks, patterns and antipatterns and is a valuable tool to evolve operations as various transformation slices are adopted and integrated. It is also useful in understanding the relationships and boundaries with the existing TOM and work that may persist within it due to regulatory requirements or risk creation reasons that may be created by changing the works delivery mechanism.

9.0   Communications and Marketing

It's a sure thing that if you don't own the messaging the messaging will own you, which is especially difficult to deal with when it's not the truth. Agile transformation is unlike other transformation in that it requires a huge amount of engagement internally with staff, to ensure that the right messages are being distributed. This messaging a is targeted at the existing structure of the organisation and facilitate adoption by customising the content around the skills of the audience. Additionally, marketing materials need to be created of visual tools to support the transformation, failing this people invent, or share from outside ones that suit their perspective creating anti-patterns in the void.

Examples of Agile Transformation Marketing Communications (Marcomms)

- agile benefits to me (target audience)
    - workers messages
    - managers messages
    - executives' messages
    - senior executives' messages
    - board messages
    - investor messages
    - analyst messages
    - unions messages
    - customer messages
- agile target operating model (ATOM)
    - agile enterprise work funding model
    - agile enterprise work definition
    - agile enterprise workflow
    - agile value slicing model
    - agile service design processing model
    - agile scaling model
    - agile portfolio model
    - agile replacement for ITIL
- agile enterprise governance model
    - agile enterprise policy creation model
- agile enterprise roles and careers definition
- agile knowledge management
- agile training directory

10.0   Advocacy and Training

There is often an imbalance between advocacy and training, this is an area where many can be put off the whole transformation. Both advocacy and training never end but they serve different purposes. This is often the area of focus of Agile Coaches, it is imperative to recognise that there are different types of coaches with different experience levels.

11.0   Planning and Implementation

At this point in the Transformation work, skills and people are separated. One of the problems in Agile in general is there are lots of different frameworks all using similar words to describe different things, I will try and help.

11.1   Behaviour and Attitude

It is essential that Agile Transformation is managed and worked on by people willing to suspend their personal and business agendas. Both these agendas will create antipatterns and build failure into the transformation. Unconscious bias often surfaces during transformation work and will affect people's experience and the overall effectiveness of the transformation. A great levelling capability for these choices is the Pasterns Board and the Transformation Steering Board mentioned in the Governance section of this book.

11.1.1 Experimentation

Avoid pre-packaged Agile Transformation they offer a compelling client story but do not tailor to the individual client company. Experimentation is the way that Agile Transformation is delivered avoid people who want to risk your company with bold launching out into the deep ideas successful transformation requires a launching out into the shallow's experimentation. Within experimentation expect to iterate what does not work to interrogate why and confirm if it is environmental, personnel or domain-based failure. Also do the same with iterations that appear to work. Never scale from a single unrepeatable experiment.

11.1.2 Interrogation

Language is very facile and can be used for good and well-intended purposes or not. Unfortunately, there are very few truths in any kind of work let alone transformation. I find appearing to be ignorant of business jargon and common processes allows me to "ask stupid questions, to avoid doing stupid things". It is also amazing the amount of hidden information that can be elicited from people if consultants would just say "I don't understand please explain". For many it's the first time their knowledge has been valued and utilised to change the working environment. Interrogate everything, seek secondary proof of everything because people often don't challenge practices or knowledge then will often believe things that are not true.

11.1.3 Evolution

Change agents by their very nature of experimentation and interrogation are changed by the environment but that is naturally filtered by various imperatives. During transformation work we must assume bias, bias in ourselves and in others. This attitude is an opportunity rather than a disability as it causes us to be evolutionary in our thinking to both adapt and be changed by what we learn while working within a transformation.

11.2   Defining the Work

It is essential to define what work actually is, it is common that the work that is required to deliver values including financial gain do not get the resources required to generate better and more outcomes. Only by defining what work is and what value it provides can a business or organisation create the correct focus of Agile Transformation.

11.2.1 Enterprise Backlog Architecture

Regardless of the primary attribute definition in your Strategic Transformation Structure it is essential that there is a commonly understood way to create backlogs at every level of your enterprise. Below is one model that shows how this works and is focused on the creation of financial value to the organisation through an alignment directly to the customer.

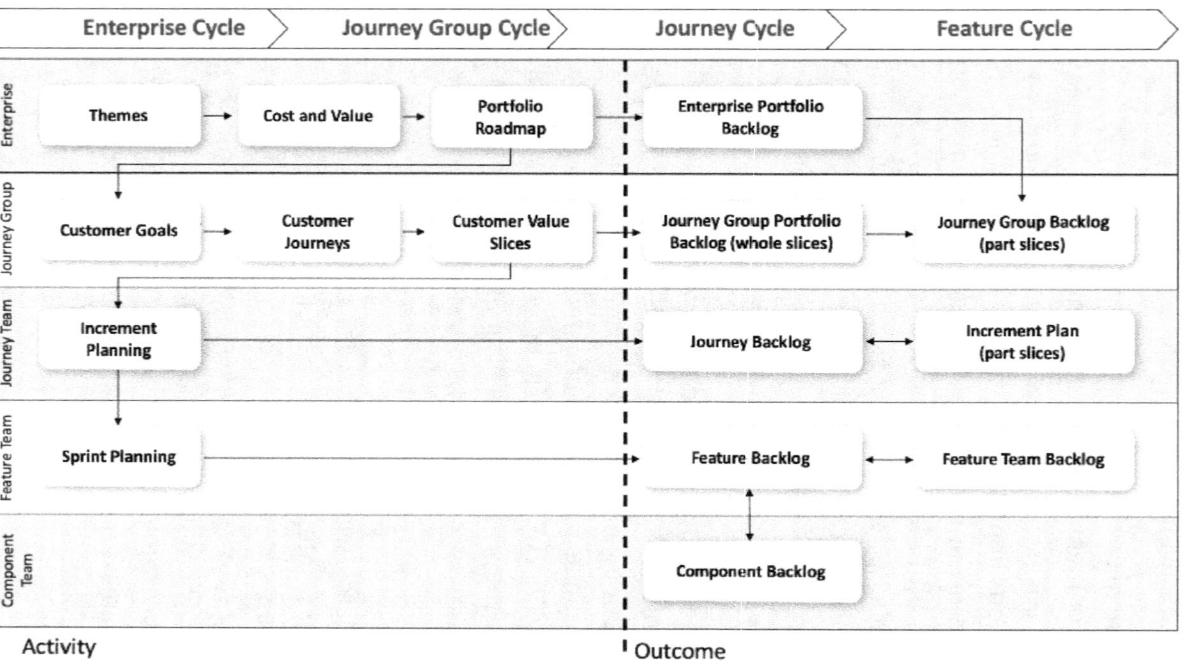

Enterprise Cycle
Journey Group Cycle
Journey Cycle
Feature Cycle
Enterprise
Journey Group
Journey Team
Feature Team
Component Team
Themes
Cost and Value
Portfolio Roadmap
Enterprise Portfolio Backlog
Customer Goals
Customer Journeys
Customer Value Slices
Journey Group Portfolio Backlog (whole slices)
Journey Group Backlog (part slices)
Increment Planning
Journey Backlog
Increment Plan (part slices)
Sprint Planning
Feature Backlog
Feature Team Backlog
Component Backlog
Activity
Outcome

11.2.2 Work Type Taxonomy

This is the critical component in defining the work and while there are common work types in most organisations regulated environment may have unique work types.

- Business initiated work
- Technology initiated work
- Regulatory work (to be defined)
- Technology maintenance and support work
- Unplanned work

1. This is a relatively straight forward process as it can be done using a simple spreadsheet for the high-level work descriptions, sponsors and planned value and outcome.
2. Next conduct due diligence over any work that cannot be brought into the transformation, due to risk, this process of prioritisation of the existing work is essential to define easily adoptable work and to create common as opposed to unique organisational design around the work. Unique work formats will be supported through flexibility in organisation design.
3. Ultimately to define the work all the actors (skills, participants, existing departments, technologies and platforms, vendors, constraints etc) must be listed, for each piece of work. This is time consuming; this time can be reduced by creating subsets of workgroups and selecting architypes

to deep dive, this does not preclude doing it for all the in-flight work eventually.

11.3   Slice Selection

It is essential that the first few slices are focused on work that delivers financial values to the organisation. This is essential to expose a commonly understood and desired outcome. It also enables a very quick view of what work does not deliver financial value and a way to start cataloguing the values of that work.

Slice selection is done by mapping several pieces of in-flight or new work using Service Design which maps the works journey (including people, processes, technologies, regulation and values). This candidate pool is then value sliced before those value slices being prioritised ~~using Weighted Shortest Job First (WSJF)~~ Economic Ordering to select the slices which will be transformed first.

I have made this sound quite easy and that it all arrives at once and is easy to understand, it's not. In a practical sense this is the puzzle part of the transformation work, it's the bit that if left unchecked by the Patterns Board (11.2.2 Work Status) can suck up all the money of a transformation. The important point here is that it is not the transformation, it is seeking and deciding by documented rationales that candidates for transformation are selected. When I do this work, I like to think I'm working on a jigsaw puzzle, what I need to understand first are the corners, if I have one already like financial value gain, then I might find customer satisfaction or marketing leading or others. Then I need the edges known technologies, people, people skills, constraints, regulation etc. Most importantly at this point I don't need the rest of the picture to gather a team of cross functional experts to value slice and then seek prioritisation through Economic Ordering.

11.4   Organise Work

ALERT if you don't do this first (for each slice) then the rest of the transformation will fail. Organising the work before defining the final organisational design or starting to organise the people is essential else, they won't be in flexible constructs that allow the correct configurations or have the viable career progression models.

Organise the work is constructed from both strategic and tactical views of the real work that is currently going through the chosen slice of the organisation.

All the following areas are involved in every slice of work that is transformed.

- Defining Enterprise Portfolio
- Defining Business Unit Portfolio
- Defining Product / Product Group Portfolio

- Defining Product / Product Group Backlog
- Defining Feature Backlog
- Defining Release Train Management
- Small Quick Wins (often through experiments)

Strategic view of work consists of the following elements,

- Book of work 1 (Golden Source, old work and candidate slices) covering business, technology and maintenance
- Book of work 2 (Golden Source, old work and completed and candidate slices) covering business, technology and maintenance
- Book of work 3 (Golden Source completed slices and old work that cannot be changes less than 5%) covering business, technology and maintenance
- Existing committed work
- Types of work
- Expected benefits and values

Tactical view of work consists of the following elements,

- Detailed view of the work before value slicing
- Value sliced detailed view of the work
- Dependencies understood

- ~~Weighted Shortest Job First (WSJF)~~
- Economic Ordering
- Agreed prioritisation
- Cost benefit
- Success measurements

11.4.1 Organise the leftover Work

There will always be leftover work that is too risky to touch that will need to be maintained in the existing format. If that is 4-5% at the end of consultancy (but not the end of the transformation) then you have been very successful indeed.

11.4.2 Work Based Organisational Design

The model below shows how the work defines the organisation.

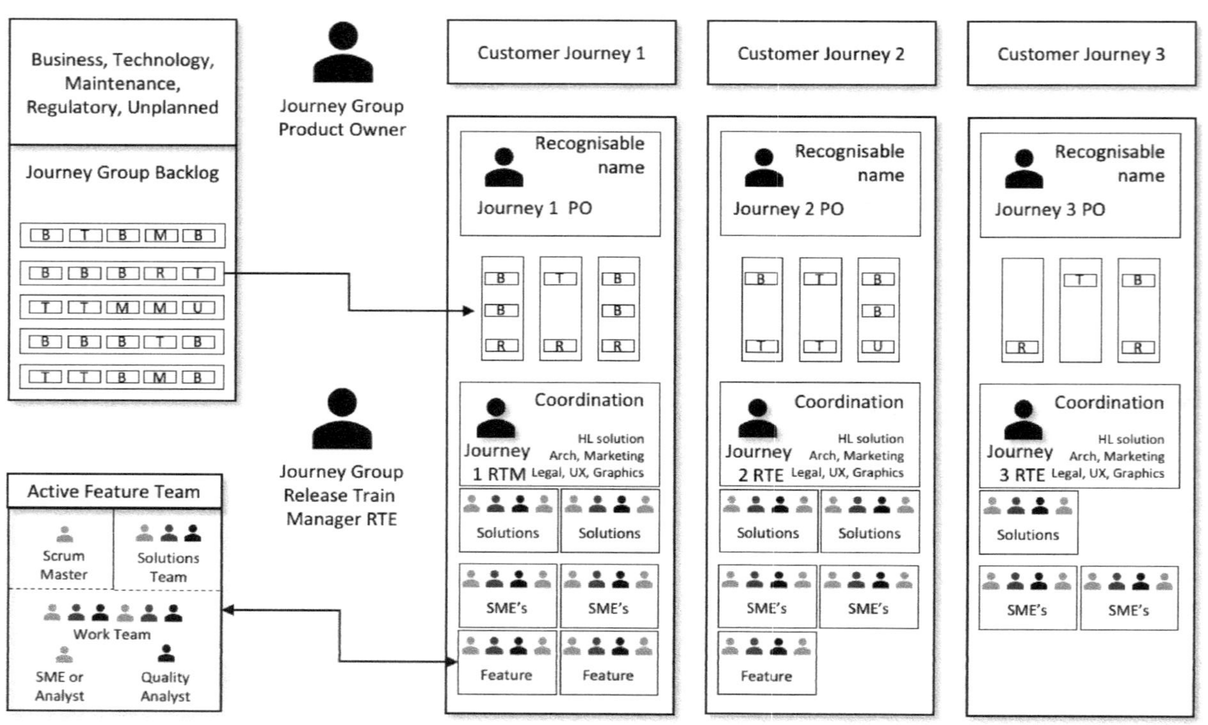

Business, Technology, Maintenance, Regulatory, Unplanned
Journey Group Backlog
B T B M B
B B B R T
T T M M U
B B B T B
T T B M B
Journey Group Product Owner
Journey Group Release Train Manager RTE
Active Feature Team
Scrum Master
Solutions Team
Work Team
SME or Analyst
Quality Analyst
Customer Journey 1
Recognisable name
Journey 1 PO
B T B
B B
R R R
Coordination
Journey 1 RTM
HL solution Arch, Marketing Legal, UX, Graphics
Solutions
Solutions
SME's
SME's
Feature
Feature
Customer Journey 2
Recognisable name
Journey 2 PO
B T B
B
T T U
Coordination
Journey 2 RTE
HL solution Arch, Marketing Legal, UX, Graphics
Solutions
Solutions
SME's
SME's
Feature
Customer Journey 3
Recognisable name
Journey 3 PO
T B
B
R R
Coordination
Journey 3 RTE
HL solution Arch, Marketing Legal, UX, Graphics
Solutions
SME's
SME's

11.5   Service Design in Agile Organisational Change

The operational side of Agile Transformation is done through Service Design as this elicits all the moving parts and affords a redesign to facilitate workflow optomisation. Since Agile is about People not Processes the persona level detail employed in Service Design facilitates the building of flexible working practices instead of the ridged structures associate with Business Process Reengineering and Business Analysis.

11.6   Test and Learn

Test and learn is a gorilla technique to quickly ascertain direction it is not the method for transformation. All test and learns are documented with a start and end date, dependencies and priority, they never state an expected outcome only a start point and measurement method. Unfortunately, I have found them to be the hiding place for scoundrels and con artists in enterprise transformations where there is no documentation provided. All test and learn documentation must be reviewable through Agile Governance.

11.7   Organise People

There is a temptation to do this in parallel before the Work has been Organised, **Don't,** you'll build inflexibility into your organisation. The primary focus is strategic to understand the skills and capabilities required to deliver the work. This requires a constant communication on the strategic level for hiring and training and the tactical for building flexibility within existing workforce.

Supporting the delivery of the work consists of the following elements.

- Planning for future work (AI, Cloud, Blockchain etc.)
- Skills required to deliver work
- Technical capabilities
- Business changes

The secondary focus is to create career packs, new common job titles and roles, however this is subject to Organise the Work being completed for each slice before the adoption of common roles (exposed in the first slice) and unique roles (exposed in the new slices). This area has constant reworking as the critical information is emergent throughout the transformation.

Another essential focus is Knowledge Management to ensure that there are records of unique skills and their attributes, practices and impact.

11.7.1 Skills Matrix

It is essential to map all the skill people have not just the ones they use in their current jobs. Further it is common to set definitions of people based upon their primary and secondary skillsets this in fact limits the success of Agile Transformation by limiting the flexibility of staff working areas, ambition and interest. I have worked on Agile Transformations that seek to encapsulate primary skills into Centres of Excellence with the intent to deliver skills guilds. Unfortunately, and uniformly people seek to convert these into organisations which ultimately cripple staff flexibility is create organisational complexity. Guilds and Centres of Excellence should be the province of Human Resources and added after the transformation is complete. They should not be part of people's job titles, career packs or advancement pathways but are a data designation based upon active and passive skills groupings.

11.7.2 Persistent Ecosystems (not just teams)

It really important that Ecosystems are created and delivered together because teams are dependent upon the quality of the materials they receive and the assets available to them to act upon the work. In the simplest sense if the portfolio requests are insane teams cannot fix that insanity only add to it. These input points need to persist, be measured for quality of inputs and be refined as do the teams, changes in input directly impact the functionality and effectiveness of teams and the delivery of value.

11.8   Scaling the Transformation

So, the term scaling is a bit misleading you can't actually scale a transformation what you need to do is absorb slices of the company into the transformation. Only by bringing new slices into a functional ecosystem is it possible to define the common or unique patterns and antipatterns of that new slice and conduct the service design required to mesh it into the already functioning slices of the business.

12.0   Governance

Governance is often seen as a limiter of Transformation however when properly engaged it becomes a great support. Like many other areas within enterprises governance is essentially a human function and those people uphold the protections for the business to stop madness from invading, disrupting and killing the organisation. It is therefore imperative to provide free (a charge code from the transformation budget) to attend training so that those involved can help design an interface between the current state, transition states and a future state of the enterprise.

12.1   Transformation to Operational Governance

The essential frame of reference for Governances is that Agile Transformation must be run using Agile. This is for two reasons,

- As training
- As a template

As training it show's in an irresistible fashion that Agile can work for an organisation. As a template it teases out the problems and areas where it can't work (or can't work at the moment), and it establishes an operating rhythm and set of commonly understood and applied activities for the whole organisation.

It is essential to recognise that Agile Governance will operate inside existing Governance until it overwhelms it by being the predominant way of working. This will only start to happen when enough organisational slices are complete that more that 50% of the organisation is operating in Agile.

12.2   Transformation Operations

It is essential that your Transformation is run like an Agile Organisation itself. Many consultancies will say it's not efficient for them to operate this way, however, why would a client think it can work for them if the transformation consultants don't use it themselves.

There are three types of transformation operations and each requires agile thinking, agile behaviours and practices that can both deliver and be built into the enterprise as BAU.

12.2.1 Transforming the work

This revolves around three key practices that are enacted across the whole lifecycle of all work. The first is planning, this planning however is not simple it requires and interconnected view from executive idea to value realisation. This is the reason to work in slices because there will be themes (new customers), epics (products upgrades), features (onboarding), stories (credit check etc.), tasks (optomise vendor contracts, align vendor development cycle etc.) in each slice.

The second is work prioritisation, although there are many ways to do this Economic Ordering provides the biggest benefits the quickest. However, like most things it requires consistent application to have value as some of the metrics are highly subjective and a common view and validation is required before agreeing any weighting. **Economic Ordering** is focused on economic benefit in many organisations though a cost of delay (CoD) divided by job size. Interestingly the same thinking can be utilised with different benefits like brand damage, share value uplift etc.

The third is enacting the plans, ensuring measurement is in place, early awareness practices, rapid escalation practices and risk, issues and blocker resolution practices are in place and functional before starting the work. This may mean setting them up and running some Fake Work through them. This will indicate the structures of the first teams needed and what their skills will be, as defined by the work. This also indicates the first work in progress limits (WIP) that are refined once real teams start working on real work.

12.2.2 Communicating the status of the work

There are a number of constructs involved in making the status of the work visible that all work on different cadences yet provide an interlocking view that support enterprise reporting. At the team level there is a daily stand-up meeting, followed by a daily Scrum of Scrums and at Enterprise level a Scrum of Scrum of Scrums. These are the essential early warning systems uniquely different from waterfall quite apart from the incremental delivery as they indicate blockers, issues and risk on a daily basis.

The weekly Patterns Board which is essential to ensure that the New Ecosystem of Patterns works together and that deviations are noted for investigation (deviations are not good or bad). This board also interfaces with existing governance and compliance usually at group level but can also engage with national or international regulators to seek guidance and support. If adjusted governance is already in place these are conversation, if not these often-become battles.

The weekly Transformation Steering Board looks at the trajectory and emergent antipatterns and establishes strategies resolution, management or for pivoting (if required). It also finds early indicators of Risk which can be investigated with an external risk team, risk management here is shown as a process box rather than a group. Patterns Approvals is shown as a process and only exists when a customer journey reaches a level of maturity to be self-organising and is evidenced by reputable metrics not just plans.

The last group the Executive Committee Board adopts the new organisational construct through Patterns Approval and Governance Approval.

It is imperative to adopt a common and transparent cadence before or as part of an Agile Transformation otherwise they will not work. "Existing cadences like quatres of the year and week numbers will underwrite any agile cadence adopted" Agile World Ecosystem Design 2007. Driving out all the cadence touchpoints from existing constructs is essential for the Agile World to work.

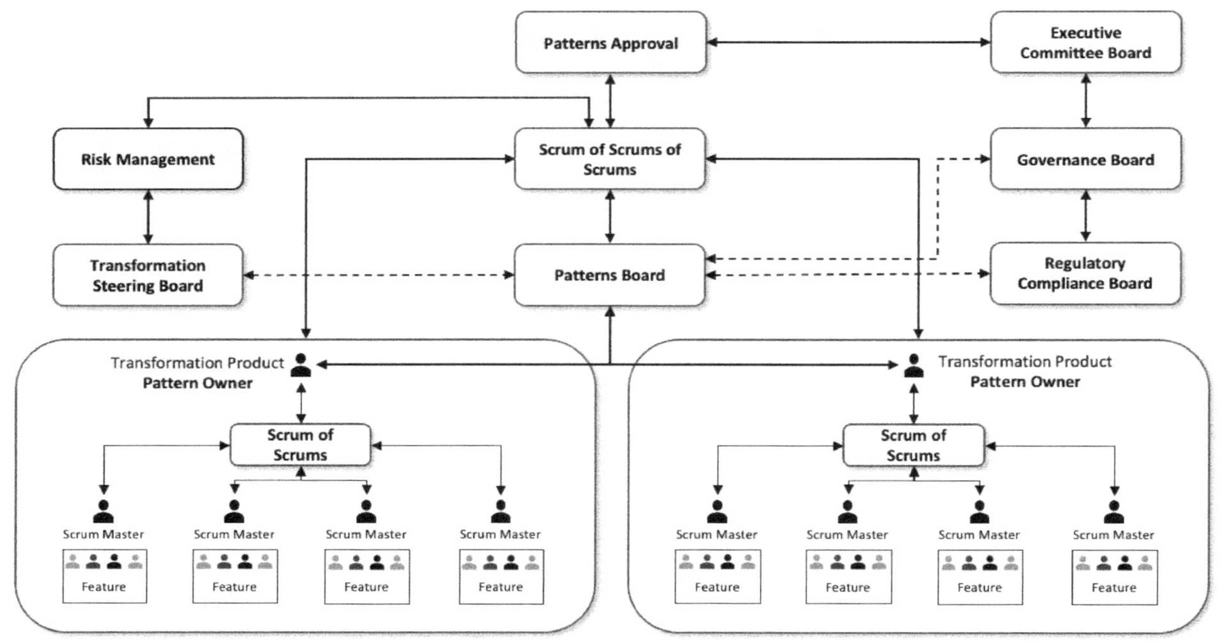

Patterns Approval
Executive Committee Board
Risk Management
Scrum of Scrums of Scrums
Governance Board
Transformation Steering Board
Patterns Board
Regulatory Compliance Board
Transformation Product Pattern Owner
Scrum of Scrums
Scrum Master
Scrum Master
Scrum Master
Scrum Master
Feature
Feature
Feature
Feature
Transformation Product Pattern Owner
Scrum of Scrums
Scrum Master
Scrum Master
Scrum Master
Scrum Master
Feature
Feature
Feature
Feature

12.2.3 Ensuring transparency around risk

Risk is a complex subject and many people in transformation and standard working prefer to not raise risks as often it has a negative impact on their work. Changing the culture around risk is essential and is built into Agile though properly run (the Scrum Master hardly talks, and the product owner is not present unless specially invited) Daily Stand-ups. The Scrum Master elicits blockers, risk and issues on a daily basis from each team members status report (they are not discussed in the meeting, unless another team member can offer a resolution). Then that conversation and the detail level is taken offline from the Stand-up meeting and investigated by the Scrum Master anything they cannot resolved immediately is reported to the Scrum of Scrums and they decide to resolve, mitigate or manage the risk. These items are minuted with the proposed course of action stated and an estimated date for completion. These minutes are available to the Scrum of Scrums as tasks and all risks are shared during SoSoS (relevant in enterprise transformations) reporting. Any risks that meet the significance criteria for the enterprise risk register are reported at SoSoS level. Only by having these communication forums can risk be discovered early and understood and an action plan made.

12.3 Definition of Done

The notion of Done is quite confusing as it means different things to different people. In software development it means done just enough to make things functional and to be tested. It's not a final done. While in business done means done forever and that it does not need reviewed unless there is a regulatory change or an incident. In agile it is the former done that is used in Agile, this single factor is one of biggest areas of contention in whole enterprise transformation and one of the greatest opportunities to optomise the business. Instead of working on large time-consuming pieces of work, the challenge for business is to adopt small just good enough work that is iterated. Only in this way can early detection of ineffectual ideas and redirection of wasted resources towards effectual ideas be made within the business.

12.4   Agile Risk Management

Agile risk management is different from existing risk management due to a number of additional attributes which include;

- Flexibility in team structures
- Concurrent working
- Iterative working
- Continuous incremental delivery

In effect Agile changes how risk management works, making it more timely but also more difficult to understand by untrained people.

Flexibility in team structures causes people to not be the owners of in-flight work but rather part of a team. The ownership moves to the product owner (for prioritisation, decisions, strategic risks and responsibility), workflow management software with data from planning, scrum, scrum of scrums, retros and metrics software covers status, dependencies, active risks, location and throughput. Depending on the Agile framework used there may also be a Release Train Engineer (RTE) essentially a Manager (often formerly PMO) who understands the interrelationships between several workflows and a wider set of prioritisation, decisions and responsibility, which in turn is serviced by a rolled-up version of the same workflow management software and metrics for RTE and Executives.

12.5   Regulatory Environments

Understandably regulated environments have difficulties that are unique in the adoption of changes in working practices and the flow of work. It may not always be possible to devolve ownership and thus accountability to teams rather than named employees. However, there are ways to make the status of work transparent so that a conversation with the regulators is not a threat to the continuance of the enterprise.

1. Brief the Regulators and what is being proposed and why and ask for their insights

(not a formal review) essentially work with them from early on
2. Provide free training for Regulators so they can see the benefits of new more transparent working practices
3. Automate workflow reporting but build in checks and balances that validate the data from a secondary source
4. Give the Regulators free remote access to workflow reporting
5. Invite the Regulators to Townhalls and Events that show the impact of transformation

12.6   Guide Rails into the Future

The primary guiderails are defined in the following chapter as part of a Ways of Working Transformation. I find describing Agile Transformation in that way to be less contentious and it removes many blockers from proponents and rejectors of Agile. It is worth noting that Ways of Working will utilise multiple Agile Frameworks and not just one and draw from other notable frameworks like Cynefin by Dave Snowdon.

The primary guiderails post external consultancy are Patterns and Antipatterns which are coalesced around organisational constructs and are the end point of the living documentation used to run the transformation work. They themselves are not static works either they should evolve also making sure to indicate common patterns, unique patterns and antipatterns. It will be natural that a bureaucracy builds up around these documents. However, it is essential that evolution is seen as normal and that responses to market moves are already supported or these patterns will become a constrictor of response instead of an enabler.

13.0   Agile Transformation for WoW

This Agile Transformation Framework takes a building block approach so that the client always has a clear line of sight on what they get for their money. Each of the following steps builds a bespoke client service, in responsive to both the experience and context of the client. Additionally, it allows for course correction as part of an iterative engagement focused on the client Subject Matter Expertise augmented by Transformation Consultants with numerous framework experiences.

13.1   Engagement

- Initial consultancy to define scope – 2 to 4 weeks to be agreed in writing prior to commencement
- Proposal presentation to refine scope – 1 to 2 weeks to be agreed in writing prior to commencement

13.2   Consultancy

The exact components and size of work will be defined during the engagement phase. All documents a living as the evolve with the transformation

- Delivery strategy using appropriate agile practices and proposing an experimental approach living document
- Benefits proposal living document
- Delivery model proposal living document
- Governance model proposal living document
- Scaling strategy living document (absorption)
- Target operating model proposal living document
- All staff HR contracts review action
- Pilot proposal for first slice document (mini experiments that build)

13.3 Delivery

- Team building – size and locations defined in consultancy
- Support document creation living document
- Training strategy living document
- Communications strategy living document

The delivery team will change over the course of an engagement in the following way;

- 2% of total team in Engagement
- 10% of total team in Consultancy
- 30% of total team in Delivery for slice 0 delivery
- 100% of total team in Delivery for scaled (see 10.8) delivery
- 30% of total team in Delivery for hand over to in house delivery teams
- 10% of total team in Delivery for hand over to in house leadership teams

13.3.1 Example

Actuals for delivery in an organisation of 90,000 people in 8 main locations globally

- 4 consultant team in Engagement
- 20 consultant team in Consultancy
- 60 consultant team in Delivery for pilot delivery
- 200 consultant team in Delivery for scaled delivery
- 60 consultant team in Delivery for hand over to in house delivery teams
- 20 consultant team in Delivery for hand over to in house leadership teams

14.0 Timeline

Timelines are subject to scope, complexity and team size the above was 2 years.

14.1.1 Client Engagement Requirements

- Ensuring an executive sponsor from your organisation is allocated to the engagement, communicates the rationale behind it, provides product ownership activities into senior leadership and signs off any 'Terms of Reference'
- Assisting in all possible ways to ensure that a contract, (and confidentiality agreement where necessary) is in place, in advance of any work commencing
- Ensuring all support is in place and access is granted for all and any required data, processes, policies, meeting rooms and nominated resources to enable successful delivery of the engagement
- Ensuring sponsor availability within the agreed timeline, to resolve any significant issues that may impact the timely completion of the engagement, if not resolved in a timely manner.

14.1.2 Consultancy Commitments to Client

- Provide support throughout service delivery using our World Class Professionals and Subject Matter Experts
- Provide high quality deliverables in a timely manner and in line with agreements upon engagement with the

client. (Any changes to this will be mutually agreed in writing, in advance, between all involved parties)
- Provide deep insights and genuine value-add in all possible areas throughout the engagement
- Provide progress updates and feedback at regular intervals, agreed in advance or at the engagement 'kick off session'
- Respect all personal and professional development of client team members throughout the engagement

14.1.3 Deliverables Ways of Working (WoW)

- WoW service design of organization
- WoW enacted service design as pilot (slice 0)
- WoW enacted service design as organisational transformation
- WoW target operating model
- WoW replacement for ITIL
- WoW enterprise work funding model
- WoW enterprise roles definition
- WoW communications
- WoW training